YOUR KNOWLEDGE HAS VALUE

AF140762

- We will publish your bachelor's and master's thesis, essays and papers

- Your own eBook and book - sold worldwide in all relevant shops

- Earn money with each sale

Upload your text at www.GRIN.com and publish for free

Bibliographic information published by the German National Library:

The German National Library lists this publication in the National Bibliography; detailed bibliographic data are available on the Internet at http://dnb.dnb.de .

Imprint:

Copyright © 2016 GRIN Verlag, Open Publishing GmbH
Print and binding: Books on Demand GmbH, Norderstedt Germany
ISBN: 9783668418370

This book at GRIN:

http://www.grin.com/en/e-book/355920/media-coverage-of-environmental-issues-in-canada-arguments-discussion

Mary Fiagbe

Media Coverage of Environmental Issues in Canada. Arguments, discussion, historical background

GRIN Publishing

GRIN - Your knowledge has value

Since its foundation in 1998, GRIN has specialized in publishing academic texts by students, college teachers and other academics as e-book and printed book. The website www.grin.com is an ideal platform for presenting term papers, final papers, scientific essays, dissertations and specialist books.

Visit us on the internet:

http://www.grin.com/

http://www.facebook.com/grincom

http://www.twitter.com/grin_com

Media Coverage of Environmental Issues in Canada

Canadian Media Coverage Evaluation

MARY MAGDALENE FIAGBE

UNIVERSITY OF WINDSOR

Index

1. Introduction

When referring to environmental issues in terms of politics, it is important to note that such issues not only affect politics, but also have an effect on the social, and economic aspects of a country, especially its people. The main goal of this research paper is to assess the media coverage of environmental issues in Canadian politics. This refers to how the Canadian media tends to frame such issues and how informed the coverage of such issues are. In order to do this, this paper is going to use four different academic readings as well as two newspapers, namely: *the National Post* and *the Globe and Mail* to evaluate the quality of such coverage. The paper in question will focus on environmental policies in the political field, especially those concerned with climate change.

Environmental policies have remained a very delicate and important part of Canadian policy for a long period of time. This is because they tend to affect the domestic and international wellbeing of the country and as such must be handled with extreme caution. This is reflected in the themes associated with the academic sources used for this paper, which will be in the first section. The body of the paper is divided into seven sections. The first four sections have to do with the main themes discussed in the academic sources, and how these themes are stated in the newspaper articles. That is, if they are covered in the articles or not. The third section examines if the newspaper articles include academic or historical facts. Next, the paper shows the extent to which academic arguments are portrayed in the articles –that is, overstating or understating academic arguments. The last section gives a summary of the paper, evaluating media coverage on environmental issues.

2. The three domestic variables

In terms of Canada's relationship with the United States in regard to the Kyoto protocol, Kathryn Harrison (2007), recognizes "three domestic variables" that determines a country's position on climate change policies, both internally and internationally. These variables include "the electoral incentives of politicians, their ideas –both causal and normative, and the institutional context".[1] These variables refer to public opinion, including their actions and insight in regards to environmental policies, the politicians' knowledge about climate change and their individual values, as well as the kind of political

---

[1] Kathryn Harrison. The Road not taken: "Climate change policy in Canada and the United States" in *Global Environmental Politics* vol. 7:4 (2007): 93.

institutions –Canada's Westminster parliamentary system, the United States' separation of power, and party discipline –present in the country, and the institutional capacity of their leaders.[2] This theme is partly covered in the *Globe and Mail article* written by Campbell Clark, taking note of the institutional capacity of Justin Trudeau during the Canadian internal climate change talks. The article mentions how the premiers of the largest provinces – including Ontario, Quebec, and Alberta, are in support of Trudeau's climate change policies. When reviewing the article, the concept of party discipline is also talked about, stating how the premiere of Nova Scotia, Stephen McNeil, took the "half-loaf of principles" mentioned by Trudeau even though he was concerned about carbon pricing.[3]

According to Harrison, (2007) Prime Minster Chrétien was able to convince his cabinet minsters that were skeptical about ratifying the Kyoto protocol by taking advantage of the parliamentary system's strong party discipline (p.112). There is also evidence of the knowledge and norm variable in the article. This has to do with the fact that, although the premiers all agreed to the fact that emissions have to be cut by 30%, and that there is a need for carbon pricing as well as emissions targets, not all of them are ready to commit to such changes or policies. A review of *the National Post* article written by Kelly McParland on March 3 also expands on this part of the theme. It mentions how the premiers of Saskatchewan and Newfoundland were against the carbon pricing policies even before the meeting took place.[4] As such, although they agree with the fact that there is a need for carbon emission policies, they are however not ready to comply with the federal government. This explains Smith's observation that "norm-building is cheap and implementation is not (as cited in Harrison, 2007, p.114)."[5] This is because they want to be able to reduce carbon emissions as they see fit –instead of a federal carbon pricing policy for the remaining states without it, they want to put their own policies in place.

---

[2] Harrison, *Global Environmental Politics*, 96.
[3] Campbell Clark, "Premiers' climate change meeting long on principles, short on specifics," *The Globe and Mail,* March 4, 2016, http:// http://www.theglobeandmail.com/news/politics/premiers-climate-change-meeting-long-on-principles-short-on-specifics/article29040659/

[4] Kelly McParland, "Premiers unite against Ottawa's carbon plan before the first gavel has banged," *The National Post*, March 3, 2016, http:// http://news.nationalpost.com/full-comment/kelly-mcparland-premiers-unite-against-ottawas-carbon-plan-before-the-first-gavel-has-banged

[5] Harrison, *Global Environmental Politics*, 114.

A review of *the National Post* article, by Jason Fekete takes note of one of the three important variables that influence a country's position of climate policies –that is the way public opinion, including voters, interest groups, environmentalists, trade unions, and businesses, influences politicians' decisions concerning climate policies. The article notes how the risk of job losses and damages to energy- intensive sectors are making the public upset about carbon price policies, especially in Saskatchewan.[6] This variable, although not enough, helps to explain why certain policies are either implemented or rejected. Strong opposition to climate change policies by some of public will be instrumental in whether policy-makers fight for a policy or not. Public opinion also helps the government to know where the public stands on a particular issue. Another important point to note is the way the media can help in shaping such public opinions. It is possible for the media to cover stories that are in favour of opposition to climate change policies. While it is true that the media can be honest in certain cases, the survival of the media, depends on them earning profit. That said there is a high probability for them to cover stories or print ads that will benefit them financial. According to Herman and Chomsky (1988), "the media's purpose is to serve the needs and interests of the elites who largely benefit from the kinds of policies that comprise neo-liberal economics –that is, the economic, social, and political interests of the elites" (as cited in Good, 2008, p.234).[7]

In instances where the resources of those opposed to certain policies outweigh that of supporters; it becomes difficult to initiate such policies. For example, Harrison (2007) mentions that in 2002, "a business community placed a series of newspaper ads across Canada, arguing that the ratification of the Kyoto protocol would put Canadian business at a severe disadvantage relative to the United States..."(p.107). This may either help some politicians in avoiding the passing of some policies, or may on the other hand make it difficult for those who want certain policies to be passed, thus affecting the other two variables. It should however be noted that such actions are not always effective. As long

---

[6] Jason Fekete, **"Environment minister pushes for carbon pricing despite worries it could 'kneecap'** energy sector," *The National Post*, February 19, 2016, http://news.nationalpost.com/news/environment-minister-pushes-for-carbon-pricing-despite-worries-it-could-kneecap-energy-sector

[7] Jennifer Ellen Good, "The Framing of Climate Change in Canadian, American, and International Newspapers: A Media Propaganda Model Analysis," *Canadian Journal of Communication,* vol 33(2008): 234.

as a leader has the institutional capacity to implement certain policies, there is a chance that it will happen. Harrison (2007) states that Prime Minister Chrétien "was able to support the ratification of the Kyoto protocol despite significant opposition from businesses and the provinces..." (p.112). She also talks about the fact that the variables influence one another by noting that Chrétien's "... conversion to environmentalism came at the end of his political career, where there was an easier tradeoff between personal values and electoral interests" (p.112).

3. Climate policy integration: Canadian federal and provincial levels

The question of who should be involved in climate change policies –federal and provincial involvement –is another important theme that is discussed in the academic readings. This is because such involvement may have both positive and negative consequences when it comes to the impact of climate change policies. When policies that are carried out by all government levels are not properly integrated or coordinated, there is the risk of higher costs (Snoddon and Wigle, 2009, p.10), higher emissions rates, implementation problems, and inter-provincial conflict. According to Snoddon and Wigle (2009):

"In Canada the climate change policy environment is currently fragmented. Both the federal government and the provinces are implementing or proposing their own initiatives, often with little thought about how they will interact with those of other governments. While multiple governments operating in the same policy field is not a unique situation in Canada, in the case of climate change this approach can be costly and environmentally ineffective..." (P.1).

As a result, the policies will become ineffective, costly and may become stagnant. Lachapelle, Borick, and Rabe (2012), add that the withdrawal of Canada from the Kyoto protocol was in part due to the disagreement between the federal government and the provincial government on what to do concerning climate change (p.344). They also address the fact that "heterogeneous sub-federal interests have produced a policy stalemate at the federal level..."(p.344).

The review of the National Post article by Bruce Cheadle points out how the federal government promised to impose a national carbon price if the provinces were unable to agree. This relates to

6

Snoddon and Wigle's (2009) statement, "a federal carbon tax can be introduced almost immediately (and, if necessary, without agreement by the provinces)" (p.18). The effects and how effective the policies or regulations will be is also pointed out in the article –" The issue is going to be, how high is that price, how tough or stringent? If the regulation is not really changing anything, the implicit price is zero." [8] The review of the articles used for this paper notes the inter-governmental conflicts that arise due to climate policy initiatives. Rabe et al (2012) stated that a number of surveys showed that "… the public places a general responsibility on the federal level, indicating that the national, state, and local governments all have the responsibility to address the issue of climate change" (p.344).

There is also the issue of how to incorporate both provincial and federal policies due to the decentralized nature of the Canadian government, where individual provinces make their own climate change policies, and also where the federal government imposes national climate change policies. The federal government may also decide to work together with the provinces to set up climate change policies. This is covered in the *Globe and Mail* article by Shawn McCarthy, stating how "Ottawa will work with industry and the provinces to establish national regulations for the sources of methane…"[9] In certain cases, the provinces adopt certain climate policies since the federal government lacks the initiative to implement them. According to Lachapelle, Borick, and Rabe (2012), one reason for support for provincial policy initiatives is due to the lack of federal engagement on the issue (p.345). They also point out that, although some people may be against "sub-federal policy initiatives" due to the "free rider problem and the issue of equity", there is still a strong support for such unilateral provincial policies (p.346). This "helps to explain the recent policy innovations undertaken by some of the provinces…" (p.346). Examples of such provinces are Quebec and British Columbia, who already have carbon tax policies (Snoddon and Wigle, 2009, p.4) and are both members of the Western Climate Initiative (WCI). Rivers (2010) also mentions the failure of the federal government to move beyond

---

[8] Bruce Cheadle, "Premiers agree to carbon pricing as part of national climate strategy," *The National Post*, March 3, 2016, http://news.nationalpost.com/news/canada/canadian-politics/premiers-agree-carbon-pricing-to-be-part-of-overall-climate-plan

[9] Shawn McCarthy, "Trudeau vows to clamp down on methane emissions," *The National Post*, March 10, 2016, http://www.theglobeandmail.com/report-on-business/industry-news/energy-and-resources/us-canada-agree-to-methane-emissions-cut-to-fight-climate-change/article29129124/

modest spending and voluntary measures to reduce national GHG (greenhouse gas) emissions levels (as cited in Lachapelle, Borick, and Rabe, 2012, p.343).

4. Canadian federal and provincial revenue sharing

Regional burden sharing and joint occupancy of the carbon tax base which are critical obstacles to moving climate change policy forward as mentioned by Snoddon and Wigle (2009) is another important theme discussed in the academic readings (p. 2 & 15). These two obstacles have to do with how the GHG mitigation policies costs are to be shared among all provinces, especially due the decentralized nature of the Canadian government. This is because certain provinces have implemented climate policies, which cause them to have high burden costs relative to those provinces with no such policy initiatives –this is referenced in the already mentioned Campbell Clark's article, stating the threat of a federal carbon price for provinces without such policies. There is as such a need for the interaction of federal and provincial policies through the implementation of a national carbon tax to reduce emissions, as proposed by Snoddon and Wigle (2009, p.2). This policy implementation will, according to them, result in revenue sharing (how to split tax revenue between the governments and share adjustments), which will be used as a "kind of lubricant to ease the economic and political costs of implementing climate change policies as well as overcoming federal and provincial resistance," (p.2). They also argue that:

"The federal government needs to retain a share of the revenues in order to reduce the political costs of imposing the tax. Provinces need a share, too; otherwise they will have no incentive to abandon their own climate change policies in favour of a more cost effective national system" (p.2).

Kelly McParland's newspaper article, which has been previously mentioned, takes note of the burden sharing and joint occupancy obstacles to climate policies. A review of a national post article, written by John Robson, partly states the implications of financial costs on public support for climate change policies. He points out that although Canadians may be in support of carbon tax policies now, that feeling will change when they realize that it is a "means of increasing revenue for governments that cant control their spending habits" –a tax grab.[10] Meaning, financial costs associated with climate change policies make public opinion less susceptible to such policies. It however fails to state wholly the theme of how the public perceives such actions by the federal and provincial governments. This refers to Lachapelle, Borick, and Rabe's unasked question on public perception of government responsibility for climate policies in federal system. This question is very important because according to Harrison (2012), public acceptability is often cited as an important condition for the enactment of stricter carbon regulations" (as cited in Lachapelle, Borick, and Rabe, 2009, p.335).

Public support of climate policies may also be influenced by "ideational contagion", where public opinion from the United States may spillover into Canada, indirectly influencing policy development (Rabe et all, 2012, p. 337). This spillover could result in delayed policy initiatives or vice versa. Good (2008) mentions that the mass media in the United States… are arguably the most prolific and influential in the world." As such, it would be very easy for its public opinion to influence climate policies in Canada –"how Canada is within the reach of the United States' massive, and influential news empire" (p.236).[11] This theme of "ideational contagion" is not referenced in any of the reviewed newspaper articles, even though it is important in determining how the public is influenced when it comes to environmental policies.

5. North American Policy regime: US - Canada climate policies

The mention of a possible "North American policy regime" in the academic readings is also covered in the newspaper articles. This is seen in the articles when they mention the talks between Trudeau and Obama's for a continental climate strategy.[12] Examples of these are the Globe and Mail articles written by Robert Fire and Shawn McCarthy. Snoddon and wiggle (2009) note that this cooperation between the North American countries does not however deter the implementation of a nation-wide federal carbon tax (p.21). This shows in the way the federal government is still pushing for a carbon tax, while

---

[10]John Robson, "The carbon tax shell game," *The National Post*, March 14, 2016, http://news.nationalpost.com/full-comment/john-robson-the-carbon-tax-shell-game

[11] Jennifer Ellen Good, "Canadian Journal of Communication", 236.
[12] Robert Fire, "Trudeau, Obama set to endorse continental strategy on climate change," The Globe and Mail, March 1, 2016, http://www.theglobeandmail.com/news/politics/trudeau-obama-set-to-endorse-continental-strategy-on-climate-change/article28991505/

at the same time trying to establish emissions reduction policies with the United States. The reviewed articles however fail to point out the implications of such cooperation. That is how it will affect the public and whether there will be support for such policies in the provinces. In regards to the policies, the newspaper articles fail to inform on the type of policies that will be implemented, especially the "market-based instruments of emission taxes and tradable emission permits, mentioned by Böhringer and Rutherford (2010, p.181).

Snoddon and Wigle (2009) make mention of a cap-and-trade system in the event of a North American policy regime. They also state that Canada is likely to use both carbon taxes and a cap-and-trade system if such cooperation takes place (p.24). The implementation of such policies are bound to improve Canada's comparative advantage, and competitiveness –relative to the United States –which were at risk following the country's ratification of the Kyoto protocol. This is because the Kyoto protocol had economic implications for Canada, unlike the US economy (did not ratify the protocol). Snoddon and Wigle (2009) explain that competitiveness was a serious concern for Canada when the United States –its major trading partner –abandoned the Kyoto protocol in 2001 (p. 14). An example of such an implication was the increase of the costs of production especially for energy intensive sectors. [13] It should be therefore noted that what happens in the United States is an important determinant of the type and content of climate policies adopted in Canada (Snoddon and Wigle, 2009, p. 14). This is especially because of the close bilateral relationship the two countries have. The reviewed articles however fail to mention this important fact.

More so, Robert Fire's article mentions a resultant improvement in "border-security measures" which is considered to be another important theme mentioned by Snoddon and Wigle (2009, p. 14). These border-security measures are imposed on goods imported from countries with less stringent climate policies (p.14). The reason for imposing such policies is to force other countries to implement strict climate change policies just like the United States, to take care of their competitive disadvantage caused by increasing business costs (p. 14). This may also explain why the Canadian government is putting for effort into making stringent emission policies on a national level. In the case where Canada

---

[13] Christoph Böhringer and Thomas Rutherford, "The costs of compliance: A CGE Assessment of Canada's Policy Options Under the Kyoto Protocol", in *the World Economy*, vol 33:2, (2010): 195.

is "judged as failing to pursue reductions with the same stringency as the US, its exporters may be subject to surcharges" –border security measures (Snoddon and Wigle, 2009, p.14).

6. Historical and Academic context of newspaper articles

In the aspect of historical and academic context, the newspaper articles have been able to state certain important academic and scientific terms, and historical references in their analysis of environmental policies, especially those concerned with greenhouse gas emissions reduction. In order to understand climate policies, their implementation and consequences, it is important to have a historical basis of information to refer to. This helps to determine how such policies are passed and also if they will be effective, while at the same time helping to make predictions about the future. The *Globe and Mail* article by Gary Mason mentions the fact that Saskatchewan's GHG emissions have grown by 66 percent from 1990 to 2013 according to Environment and Climate Change Canada.[14] This historical fact is important because it informs the public of the possible level of emissions in the said province as well as the need of stringent emissions policies in the province –resulting in high public support for environmental policies, and a temporary solution for the low level of public attention to climate change issues.

Another important academic context in the newspaper articles have to do with the current emission levels in the provinces and Canada as a whole, and the fact that Canada and the United States are large emitters of methane gas –GHG gas (Shawn McCarthy, March 10, 2016). This information helps to peak public interest in climate policies, which helps to influence the federal and provincial governments' commitment level to climate change. Carbon pricing is also an academic context used in the newspaper articles' analysis of environmental issues. The term –carbon pricing –noted as a wondrous market mechanism in Terence Corcoran's article serves as a means by which GHG emissions levels are to be reduced.[15] It also helps to inform the public about the possibility of a national

---

[14] Gary Mason, "Why Justin Trudeau's climate change policy is an impossible dream," *The Globe and Mail,* March 4, 2016, http://license.icopyright.net/user/viewFreeUse.act?fuid=MjE5ODg3NDc%3D

[15] Terence Corcoran, "The great green carbon tax grab," *The National Post*, February 25, 2016, http://search.proquest.com.ezproxy.uwindsor.ca/docview/1768095632?accountid=14789

carbon tax to aid in emission reductions as well as the estimated costs and prices associated with these policies. The cap-and-trade system is also another climate change policy mechanism. These two mechanisms inform the public about what measures policy-makers are planning to implement for climate change. Robert Fire's mention of the United States' border-security measures and the significance of Prime Minister Trudeau's invitation to the United States' state dinner are academic and historical contexts that are important for climate change policies or initiatives. In order to elaborate on this significance, Fire mentions the fact that Canada hasn't been invited to the US state dinner since 1997, when Jean Chrétien was invited by Bill Clinton, until now. This historical context helps to explain the recent important cooperation between both leaders –Trudeau and Obama –and how such cooperation will affect climate change policies on a continental scale.

Campbell Clark's article (March 4, 2016) also contains a historical context through the comparison of the "Canadian internal climate change talks" in Vancouver to "International summits" on the same issue. He also compares the kind of influence and power the Prime Minister has to that of the United Nations. This influence will help in determining the success of climate policies by the federal government led by the Prime Minister. This therefore makes it an important point to note, especially when provinces (for instance Saskatchewan and Alberta) are against certain federal climate change policies. This historical comparison also shows the impact of international policies on Canada, not forgetting the use of vague international climate principles, which need to be thoroughly explained in order to make policy implementation less complicated.

7. Portrayal of academic arguments in newspaper articles

From the overall analysis of the articles and academic reading, it is safe to say that there are traces of understatement of academic arguments. When talking about public opinion, the articles make note of the consequences of climate change policy to the public –including job losses (as seen in Jason Fekete's article). It however understate how the public influences climate policies, that is what will happen to policies when public opinion is for or against them, and how involved the public are in climate policies. Thus, the articles only talk about the consequences, while forgetting public knowledge and impact on such policies. As such, it only mentions one aspect of public opinion –consequences – while giving no attention to how the public can influence climate policies. Another example is when John Robson (March 14, 2016) states in his article that Canadians may change how they feel about carbon taxes when they realize that it is simple a tax grab (increasing government revenue through taxes). The article however fails to show how the public could react to such a realization –except by lowering support. Thus, the articles understate the academic argument of public opinion.

On the issue of market mechanisms for emissions reduction, the articles tend to be more focused on carbon tax mechanisms (overstate), giving little attention to the other market mechanism of cap-and-trade. Emphasis is therefore placed on carbon pricing as the prevailing means of reducing gas emissions, while putting other mechanisms including, emissions trading permits and technology funds on the side. Such mechanisms are therefore understated in the newspaper articles. John Robson's article is an example of this situation. It points out the need for carbon taxes to discourage gas emissions, the estimated total amount of carbon taxes as well as how the tax revenue may be used (for example, "investing in green projects"). It however fails to mention other emission mechanisms that may be used or are already in use in the country –some provinces are working to implement a cap-and-trade system for emissions reduction. When taking the market mechanisms into consideration, the newspaper articles talk about Canadian and US joint efforts to impose certain climate policies, but they do not mention which kind of mechanisms may be used in this continental cooperation strategy. Robert Fire for example, only makes mention of an "environmental and climate-change package" in his March 1, article. Even though the academic argument of a North American policy regime is noted, there is little information about what that policy regime may entail in respects to the market mechanisms for emissions reduction – carbon pricing and emission permits (cap-and-trade system).

In addition, the newspaper articles also tend to overstate federal climate change policies compared to provincial ones. Although there is mention of provincial climate policies especially carbon tax in Quebec and British Columbia, the articles understate such policies. It is true that national climate policies are very important for Canada's efforts in GHG reduction, however, the articles tend to focus more on national policies that are to be put in place by the federal government, as opposed to regional policies. They are as such not fair in their portrayal of the academic argument of federal and provincial involvement in climate policies (they overstate federal policies and understate regional ones). An example of this is seen in Shawn McCarthy's article where he makes note of how the federal government –he calls it "Ottawa" –will work with the provinces to set up national regulations for methane sources. This further explains how both Canada and the United States are working to regulate methane gas emissions. The article also slightly mentions Alberta's climate plan, but it is noted that this mention was to state how the provisions in the plan is to help in determining Canada's overall approach to climate change policies on the federal level (nation-wide). It is however important to talk about both sides —federal and provincial —because Canadians generally believe that all government levels are responsible for climate change initiatives. Also there is the need for an integration of both federal and provincial climate change policies in order to enable Canada get far in its goal of emissions reduction. With respect to this academic argument, the newspaper articles try to cover all sides, but are not fair in their portrayal of the issue since they overstate one aspect and understate the other.

8. Conclusion

The overall reference to the academic readings and the evaluation of the newspaper articles, show that media coverage of environmental issues is usually based on climate change policies. Also, the media makes an effort to cover certain important themes that influence climate change policies. This includes public opinion, electoral incentives, individual knowledge and values (norms), and institutional capacity. Further more, the media coverage of such issues tend to incorporate both the federal and provincial governments, their level of authority and influence, discussions, and how they work in achieving climate policies —including the use of carbon taxes and other climate initiatives. The media also places importance on the joint efforts by both the United States and Canada to implement a continental strategy for solving environmental issues, especially those affecting the climate. That said, the use of both historical and academic context in news coverage of environmental issues shows how much effort the media puts into their discussion and analysis of climate issues.

Even with the negative aspect of overstating and understating certain academic arguments, the coverage of environmental issues —which is considered to be a very important aspect of human life —in terms of Canadian politics, is far better that average. On that note, media coverage of these issues could be given a score of 7 out of 10, in a ratings survey. To make up for the lost points, media coverage on such issues in terms of Canadian politics should be fair and clear without giving more emphasis to one side while understating or ignoring other sides. There also needs to be more information on the advantages of climate change policies, instead of the regular focus on the negative consequences of environmental policies.

9. Bibliography

Lachapelle, Erick; Borick, Christopher P.; Rabe, Barry. "Public Attitudes toward Climate Science and Climate Policy in Federal Systems: Canada and the United States Compared 1." Review *of Policy Research*, 29(3), (2012): 334-357.

Harrison, Kathryn. "The Road not taken: Climate change policy in Canada and the US." In *Global Environmental Politics* vol. 7:4. (2007): 92-117.

Böhringer, Christoph, and Rutherford Thomas. "The Costs of Compliance: A CGE Assessment of Canada's Policy Options under the Kyoto Protocol." In *the World Economy* vol 33:2, (2010): 177-211.

Cheadle, Bruce, "Premiers agree to carbon pricing as part of national climate strategy." *The National Post*, March 3, 2016, http://news.nationalpost.com/news/canada/canadian-politics/premiers-agree-carbon-pricing-to-be-part-of-overall-climate-plan

Clark, Campbell, "Premiers' climate change meeting long on principles, short on specifics." *The Globe and Mail,* March 4, 2016, http:// http://www.theglobeandmail.com/news/politics/premiers-climate-change-meeting-long-on-principles-short-on-specifics/article29040659/

Corcoran, Terence, "The great green carbon tax grab." *The National Post*, February 25, 2016, http://search.proquest.com.ezproxy.uwindsor.ca/docview/1768095632?accountid=14789

Fekete, Jason, "Environment minister pushes for carbon pricing despite worries it could 'kneecap' energy sector." *The National Post*, February 19, 2016, http://news.nationalpost.com/news/environment-minister-pushes-for-carbon-pricing-despite-worries-it-could-kneecap-energy-sector

Fire, Robert, "Trudeau, Obama set to endorse continental strategy on climate change." The Globe and Mail, March 1, 2016, http://www.theglobeandmail.com/news/politics/trudeau-obama-set-to-endorse-continental-strategy-on-climate-change/article28991505/

Good, Jennifer E. "The Framing of Climate Change in Canadian, American, and International Newspapers: A Media Propaganda Model Analysis," *Canadian Journal of Communication,* vol 33. (2008): 233-255. http://www.cjc-online.ca/index.php/journal/article/view/2017

Mason, Gary, "Why Justin Trudeau's climate change policy is an impossible dream." *The Globe and Mail,* March 4, 2016, http://license.icopyright.net/user/viewFreeUse.act?fuid=MjE5ODg3NDc%3D

McCarthy, Shawn, "Trudeau vows to clamp down on methane emissions." *The National Post*, March 10, 2016, http://www.theglobeandmail.com/report-on-business/industry-news/energy-and-resources/us-canada-agree-to-methane-emissions-cut-to-fight-climate-change/article29129124/

McParland, Kelly, "Premiers unite against Ottawa's carbon plan before the first gavel has banged." *The National Post*, March 3, 2016, http:// http://news.nationalpost.com/full-comment/kelly-mcparland-premiers-unite-against-ottawas-carbon-plan-before-the-first-gavel-has-banged

Robson, John, "The carbon tax shell game." *The National Post*, March 14, 2016, http://news.nationalpost.com/full-comment/john-robson-the-carbon-tax-shell-game

Snoddon, Tracy, and Wigle, Randall. "Clearing the Air on Federal and Provincial Climate Change Policy in Canada." *Institute for Research on Public Policy*. (2009): 1-24. http://irpp.org/research-studies/choices-vol15-no11/